The Arrangements

Also by Kate Colby

I Mean
Blue Hole
The Return of the Native
Beauport
Unbecoming Behavior
Fruitlands

The Arrangements

Kate Colby

Four Way Books
Tribeca

Library of Congress Cataloging-in-Publication Data

Names: Colby, Kate, author.
Title: The arrangements / Kate Colby.
Description: New York, NY : Four Way Books, [2018]
Identifiers: LCCN 2018003716 | ISBN 9781945588211 (pbk. : alk. paper)
Classification: LCC PS3603.O419 A6 2018 | DDC 811/.6--dc23
LC record available at https://lccn.loc.gov/2018003716

This book is manufactured in the United States of America and printed on acid-free paper.

Four Way Books is a not-for-profit literary press. We are grateful for the assistance we receive from individual donors, public arts agencies, and private foundations.

This publication is made possible with public funds from the New York State Council on the Arts, a state agency.

PROUD MEMBER

We are a proud member of the Community of Literary Magazines and Presses.

Contents

The One

The Burial

Things go together because they *are* together.

—Kate Greenstreet

The One

Inside Job

The difference between
shade and shadow is

the former you inhabit.
The difference in

magma and lava is
the same to the core.

I've inspired some
love songs, but never

a history text, please
write me back, I'm

dying, you
see, the thing is

shadows can't be black
when they're made of light.

Middleman

Only the body dies, but
it takes the rest with it.

Whether the rest is then
dead or forever

inaccessible is immaterial.
Day breaks into nets, entangles

air between birch and fence,
the trellis and the rose.

We meet in the middle
with words to render

myself unnecessary
and invincible. But sites

are trained and vines
espaliered—splayed, still

shivering in the web,
I'm not immortal yet.

View

I'm the would-be sort
who throws up windows

to welcome morning,
but at 4:45 the crows

get going in gray light
weakening around

the shades. The chain-
link city rattles its chains.

Because the counter-
weights are broken, I

prop it open with a crowbar.

Half Bad for Almost 40

Earlier I walked in a meadow.
I know because it said so on the sign.

Old bees bumped in the goldenrod,
shafts of chaff cast Queen Anne's lace

into its florets, and those into theirs,
like fractals.

Crab apples have fallen
into, anachronistic in the privet.

(Increasingly, I get confused with the world.)

A perfect medium belongs
to both sides, like a window.

Viz. bees buzz through me,
but bump against the panes.

Platform

Form follows shape
of the tool, but any

similarity between
them is incidental,

unless hands drawing
hands, and so forth.

*

Nothing pre-exists words
to remember with or else

time immemorial is
a memory in and of itself.

My mother used to ask,

*How much do you charge
to haunt a house?*

*

Words are circular
saws designed

to cut straight lines,
turned on their sides,

they pound out poems
after themselves, stacks

of pallets holding
only one another.

The One

There's no such thing
as an imaginary circle.

Even weather is spherical.
We are vacuum-packed

in atmospheres, sensory
and insensible, making eyes

for how I want you, this
dark room, bright screen—

we are all too great
and small to see

the thinnest air
I can't breathe.

Strand

Between the ghost
in the machine and

the built-in obsolete,
my head is inclined

to the sun in my eyes.
A Capri Sun packet

flashes in the rocks,
upstaging the waves,

bendy straw bent into
cleaving saxifrage.

I'm of two minds about
bodies. Within or with-

out you, what needs
to be there before you

can see it—searing sun
spots on the back of my

hand, the one I know so
well, next to nothing.

The System

Book covers
curl, shaker

caked with salt
humidity—

I can't speak for
thinking of you

St. Francis, hand
aloft in the garden

here you are here you are here you are.

My daughter collects buttons in a box
whose only purpose is containing them
while their purpose is being contained.

X-ing out the window panes,
collecting non-perishables

watching it rain in the ocean.

Green Blind

Sea grapes draped
on split-rail fence,

a cart track to the
settlers' graveyard.

Chipped, unnamed
baby graves, black

with mold, old lichen,
those phrases like fire

lanes through language
—I love you—

black hole left by
stone thrown into

otherwise intact
algal mat.

Stoup

Mace offsets the sweetness
and mustard's for emulsion;

acid cuts the salt,
sugar the heat;

coriander adds complexity
and chocolate tames the chilies.

The roux or the meat,
the fallen bone, this

sour starter's moldered
for upwards of a century.

There's so much light
I can't stand.

How much I don't know
I don't know.

Bulletin

I want to be inside of
what I only displace—

night, sunlight, the sea
swallow me, but only

into a slow dissolve
between. If I could

fade out, un-
fast to black,

I'd know the volume
of darkness. As it is

I'm an empty pin-
board full of pins.

Bog Star

The better part
is taken, time

and again, now
let me see—

rusty green over-
passes, white sky

grass of Parnassus,
which is neither

grass nor Greek. C'mon,
man, give me the keys.

In the median strip
convicts stab trash

with sharp sticks.

Exhibit A

You are always born
in your birthplace,

but it's rare to die
on your grave.

I take up space
like a habit—

nothing matters
and branches

the color of their
shadows on snow.

In white noise, no
silence (*death-*

place is a word),
a poem is there

to understand
its origin.

The Beholder

Were we born with eyes
or when we saw ourselves

seeing? Space is limit-
lessly visible and still

my vision excludes me.

They warned of black ice
on the roads this morning—

black meaning unseeable
notwithstanding its sheen.

Beauty's meaning is
its appearance, fusion

of seer and seen
confused with love

the only thing between us
is the room we take up.

Two Sentences

"Weeds" is missing
words for outdated

vegetation—"fescue,"
"feverfew" and "sedge."

If I displaced all particulars
of me with the category you

fall into, Tess d'Urberville,
self-effacing in the swede

field (only I'd call them
"rutabagas"), then kill

and hang for my own name
but call it love—small price

to pay for having it thus.

Then-Wife

Everything is an omen but doesn't know it,
which is the opposite of the Butterfly Effect

since things don't always have to have happened.
In hindsight, everything is an omen of everything

that comes after it, regardless of cause.
Or regardmore. There, I've coined it.

Everything has been coined at some point—
words and what they stand for. With eyes.

Also, things don't any less have happened
the further in time you get from them—

even memories only ever happened
right now. I was once in a room so hot

and crowded that our sweat condensed
on the ceiling and rained back down.

I think of this every time
I walk beneath a dripping

window unit.

Boxing Day

In light of
this weakness—

sort-of blood
orange, but no

heart in it—hands
fall from what

I cannot tell
time: pitch

    pine, twisted
    black cathedral

(sun fell down the day
at Chichen Itza).

I hold to the bone
and the medium,

skin breaking into
its own, so to speak

to the night,
this circum-

scribed horizon—
what I mean

to leave there.

The Arrangements

A photo is mostly finished,
but you can't consummate

a painting in time. The eyes
will follow till one of you is

nearly exhausted or a head
in a crested conquistador hat

appears from behind the holes.
It grins. You die. No, lie

next to me while I grind
through the night. I want you

to hold my hand across a rough
surface and read me this song,

but you have to get the words wrong.

Dregs of the season
depend from the trees,

wet mats of leaves
still being rained on.

Loathe this cold
but hold it close,

let it get colder, as
things you intend

to tell but won't.
Apparent absence

is presence enough
for the moment.

I will say this much
for silence

to break it
is to know

what holds us
here
to the bone.

Broken down
on the road

from you,
red mist

of budding trees
a clump of

dead sumac, I think
to say the least.

Day doesn't so much
progress as condense—

rain fills red Solo bowls
for feral cats in the yard.

If life could be saved
I'd take the lump sum

meaning all at once
after the beep on my

answering machine:

Petals pour down
the street to the bay.

See what I'm saying?
It looks like a mouth.

Steam curls from hosed
concrete, thick silence-

studded finches,
crosswalks stutter

cut here—

nothing's clear
enough to see through.

Invisible windows
come between

and seem the same.
Beauty's useless

afternoon moon,
a complete hole

into which
the eye grows

its pupil.

Are hours consumed or
do they accumulate?

Time is a trash bag
forever collecting itself.

My cup, quenched
teeth, clenched

fist, screaming
into it—

will you listen to
that mouth on you

blowing trick candles
you can't self-extinguish.

To think you don't get to see
your own innards, the number

of breaths (do they even
have a value if uncounted?)

Time exists if you buy it.
You crank it out like an awning

and stand under it. Or don't.
Standing next to it is not

an option, though. (Just try
to go around a river.) I try

to experience my entrails, can't
sleep for containing them. Is this

the same or opposite as being
in the world without eyes for

the infinite?

Homing

I draw curtains
across what

I can't see

I want nothing
so badly

to take place
like a pill

live in this
lit circle

falling on thresholds
without doors

rooms I know
are there

still.

Poem

This is a poem about a time of day
when the light still seems to mean it,
but shadows from roofs and other
pitched, impermeable things
have begun their colonial sweep.

This is a poem about a time of year
when clear, high-pitched light,
ungolden but suggesting warmth
makes the brown, brittle rose vines
look suddenly far from soulful.

This is a poem about a time of life
when one lets go all at once
of regrets, since their sources
are remote and one no longer
does anything worth regretting.

This is a poem about inception,
resignation, no bees and no clean
white snow, rather these dirty dregs
with old tennis balls frozen into them.

No. This is a poem about everything that is
not this poem, including this poem. Well,
I'll be. There is no time here, now
let the dog in, go wash your hands.

The Burial

Pine

There's a first time
for everything and

now we're in for it.
Sheet lightning

keeps striking, splits
this susceptible trunk

in two. Gather a few
wind-bruised needles

to preserve in pages,
winch me back into

a passable intactness,
forever accidentally

waiting to happen.

Theory

The world is everything
in this case—bare limbs

before day, all gray,
parts and parcel of

their own pieces, see-
through or too small

not to see around.

I looked at the sun one time,
saw the vessels of my eyes.

Can't see
why, just so

I don't think
as far as I know.

Beauty Contest

A sunset is moving
because you can see

the sun is moving
away. My heart

in my throat and
beating, luffing

toward bloody rim
of unknown, no

made of distance.
(A circle doesn't

have to have
circumference.)

Everything
at some quantity

is poisonous, even
beauty's still

more toothsome ruin.

Through the unseemly
rip in my paper gown,

my crown, remains
to be seen.

Métier Pants

Cooks wear checks
to hide their messes.

Painters' pants are white
to highlight their own.

Why this difference in what
we want to know of business?

The cost of what you're willing
to put where your mouth is.

I'm always talking about language
leading to palliative thinking

like a horse to drink.
Oh, and jodhpurs

with seamless crotches
to protect from wear—

I wear my white legs bare
with Wite-Out.

Inlet

A skin of ice
will melt through

morning; the sea is
seeping back into it-

self. Brittle grass
behind glass at the

end of my eyes,
my body begins

to break into it.
There's so much

here to work with.
A head is home-

sick, as though
ice were only

there to hold
the water in.

Asarotum

Nothing will not
happen eventually.

Frigid light slices
through ivy, old-

timey garbage now
paved at Haymarket.

Time is retro-
viral, gifting it-

self in remnants—

bronze corncobs,
staves, soda tabs.

But bridging a gap
does nothing for

the gap.

Yours Truly

I can't see light at the end
of this blinding tunnel

until I cover my hand with
my eyes. A slack tide's

brown leaves pack against
the breachway. Some plastic

trash is in it. Two wind-
bent men watch a severed

red-and-white fishing bob
bobbing away. If/when

"over" means "forever,"
I need you to possess me,

not like "occupy,"
but "empty."

Promise

A treasure chest rests on
the bottom of the tank

its lid shooting up
and then drifting back down

to close again
on the promise of content:

it's bottomless
with a garish gravel in it.

*

That there's
so much here

means the world
you see

gnat-black
dusk falls

through floor
to ceiling

windows.

*

How far I've come
into my own

promise kept
rather than shown

all I've done
so far

from what I know.

Overhead

Time is no longer
than a breadbox

but it weighs more
on this scale—what

unit of shape on the
face of it is ticking?

Contents have shifted,
I am traveling light

this morning—

thin trees, stripped
phalanges indicate

still water on which
they are imprinted,

billows in duplicate
from the hospital

incinerator—smoke
becomes the cumulus

unless it's a boiler.

Cure

I did not think
to ask for this
                    •

kind of light—

weak in the leaves
            buckled to the ground

so much distance
and nothing in it,

not mine to give
or get rid of.

Sowing words in waste
of borrowed space, they

grow a circle around me
come summer, salt-filled,

now whose small bones
I pick with a thin knife.

Castaway

A wracked strand
of egg-sac entrails

cochlear seashells
I hold to my ear

what holds it here:
an ebbing at the center.

I have a white flag
built into my skin

to give in to what
I turn again—

Noah's wife watching
her friends float by

face down in God-
forsaken flotsam:

Red Nun

I take up so much room
I can't go back into.

Superscape bleeds through—
corroded water towers, fire

escapes, billboard holders.
You know, overpass fencing

is less for jumpers
than throwers. I didn't

and what difference there
is taking place before me—

salt-eaten barge
red right returning

to the scrapyard, where infra-
information emerges in pilings

reduced by waves and weather.
I mean the wind and water is

the amount by which they're
diminished. At least half.

Lodged in the black,
dry weeds, a vanilla

cigarillo package.

Piece

Space is there
to be expanded into.

Here's a municipal
cleanup crew, power-

washing the overpass.
A bed sheet billows

about their heads:

WELCOME
HOME PVT
MARTINEZ

Nonce space taking
place before you—

a vacuum only
moves one way

from the room
to be taken up.

Wistless

In-your-face blooms
now brown, drooped

into black
eyes of dying Susans.

Hosta and helio-
trope don't go,

but in time, do
coexist, you

imperfect word.

Screen door squeaks,
buffeting whump of

unfast ceiling fan.
Summer throes, all

my unrequited silence is
quiet, a quality of noise.

Error Message

This tin-
tinnabular cold,

fragile light to
shatter through

branches, hairline
fractures in blue

screen between
my eyes and me,

so close to being
what I make

happen to see.

Radiator

As ice numbs the pain
of its own application,

so, too, this swollen
sun on the lip of it.

I've had a rich life:

went to school, had two
kids, got a tattoo, then

removed it. Acronyms
grow into themselves,

like "laser," and "save"
can mean keep or deliver,

the smell of heat from
my sibilant radiator

just now keeps me
safe as sound.

Look Out

The idea of mountains
older than mountains

taking place
before me.

Peak season, one
week before I turn

forty, bittersweet
berries burst in on

their innards,
cadmium splats

eclipse the canvas.
Days get numbered

later, but from
here I can see

where echoes go
to die behind me.

Dead Reckoning

I see with you in silence
the volume of speechlessness—

to say nothing of speech—
how differently we seem.

Like afterlife and dreams,
if it's real till you're in it,

do you sleep even?

Distance deafens
difference between

fake logs and real fire.
If my face feels weightless

it's not for lack of having
thought that far.

Bad Star

History is in the making—
ghost-white Indian pipe

goes black beneath
white ash, tangled

mats of morning glory
list the rotten pickets.

Here lies devoted wife,
mother, daughter (will

the brightness invert,
like constellations from

the other side?) Time
has no contemporary,

my epitaph-*à-trois* is
written. I use sealant

to deter the worms—
a broken couplet still

a unit.

The Plunge

Black evergreens
pre-dawn, it's all

there before you
just don't exist

until you're in it.
Not blind to finery

of felt darkness, what
I wouldn't do for you—

pick love like splinters
of light from the light

leave slivers of night
these words fall into.

Remains

For Darcie Dennigan

It's taking so long
this time

at the end of my eyes

to be discontinuous,
at least to believe it.

Once I climbed what's known
as the first dune of the Sahara

(despite how many there
must be at the periphery),

rose from nowhere.

Time was a sophisticating
form of darkness; it was

then I built this
fortress, the walls

of which date back
at me.

Prospect

Ice caul over air-
locked puddles,

discarded trees
line the street.

Crowning sky
stars the night

before me,
clerestory—

of all windows
to see this through.

Reflection on an Indoor Pool

Steam rains
down the windows.

Snow falls in
its tracks.

We talk of "flow," but unlike
water, words have no sound—

to speak is not to know
or have them, but crack

a beefeater, make him laugh.

He'll go home to
his reparative wife,

defrosted lasagna,
yesterday's news.

Bad Crucible

Raw sidewalk piled up
with corner-store carnations,

conic plastic, *RIP Sweet Angel.*
Remember Johnny Tremain,

his fingers fused together
by molten silver? Bad scene.

Boring historical fiction.
I have a chronic condition:

when the time comes
that my head goes

before this skin of
impassive glass,

shattered silver-
side out.

Broad Night

The only light is
all around—full

moon on each
ice-locked twig,

reflective mess
with brutal stars

in it. Love
is distance

its reaches
in your face

branching there.
Here chandelier

of dependent prisms,
what nimbus splits

into and joins it.

Croatoan

What I wouldn't give
for the world—this

last word in lost tracks,
black trunks listing

in the intermittent
swamps of spring.

Useless, useless,
said John Wilkes Booth

regarding his time
drawing near

what is is
being heard here.

The Curse

The first morning on Earth
dawned on what yesterday

was too small or not round
enough to have a horizon.

Darkness was introduced
and now there's even more

room to be removed in—
cross-hatched penumbra,

clipped moon, a stripe
of light under the door.

A view can be long
or dim or of Delft,

but it takes its time
to draw the night

Overextended

As though we'd cross
our borders when there

are armed men
and barbs. Turn

back to the interior
of bones, bleached

femurs. As seams
of metal and minerals

hold together and
asunder the Earth,

I'll see you not
if I see you first.

Sound

Breaking waves
unbroken sound

whose syllable
I can't speak to.

The life left
in little deaths

of inexactness—
the shape

of the wind
ungathering asters.

My perimeter is
what puts me here

my volume
made of sound

as night is made
of dark and light

mosquitoes feed
this evening out.

Restoration

Whittled bone-
shaped bone—

words won't keep
more than you think.

Across the street
a sheet of black

Tyvek house wrap
slaps in the breeze,

a glimpse of pine
siding with its stand

amid the deciduous.
Death is resurrected

daily from flesh,
but for how long

does a vacated body
retain its name?

Old beams
fold home.

The Burial

Never to be outdone by woods,
where you heard the rain before

feeling it—now is the time

to weave wreaths from waves'
graven mats of marshweed.

Please bear with me
this pall of pressed-

tin, skim-milk sky;
to this day I don't speak

but wake up three feet under
with blindness of bright snow.

Don't want to go out
in it.

*

Things I miss about living
in cities: dark shafts, cinder-

block backs of places,
stringy saplings staked

in squares of dirt and dog
shit with cups in it.

Now time is served in slow
pixelated shapes beholden

only to their deliquescence
building behind the window—

snow on sand, its dissonance.

How could I hold a candle to
what I would melt all over with.

*

"Salt box" is the shape named for
a tool we no longer use or would

even recognize, but a whispering
wall, bridge of sighs, architecture

of what the head is
too full not to hold—

how pleasing, all this
work to be put there.

funny little A-frame, you
funny little A-frame

The work is trying
to end with my eyes

to die in time
to spare myself

only sounds like you
will survive this winter.

*

Kleenex shreds in the dryer,
contents of the kids' pockets

banging through the morning
a bowl of banana stickers, your

everyday near-death experience.
Long for this world, I am out-

performing water, light,
closing night, house

to black—

a hothouse overgrown
with underbrush,

the cost of thinking
this much.

To Be Continued

Shrill light from snow
yellows in the window

a frizzle of dead
baby's breath.

Everything is one of a pair
except collectively—nope

goes with nothing.

The "original" begat
everything since

also what's never
happened before—

I can't exist
any/more.

Annunciation

See, at the beginning of
the painting she cradles

her viscera, a small window
hovering in front of her

head. By the end, this
tentative angel has taken

from her the purpose of
history, to hold together

more than one horizon.
I can't give back the time

I've taken up, but return
my capacity to the air,

alveoli to the vine, turn
myself in to eyes.

Acknowledgments

Thank you to the editors of the following journals and series, in which some of these poems previously appeared: *A Perimeter, Boneless Skinless, Boog City, Sink Review, The Volta, Pallaksch. Pallaksch, PEN America,* and *Sixth Finch.*

A portion of this book was published as *Engine Light,* a chapbook from PressBoardPress, for which I am grateful to Patrick Reidy.

For various forms of support, friendship, advice and conversation critical to this work, thank you to Mary-Kim Arnold, Lee Ann Brown, Mónica de la Torre, Joanna Howard, Caroline Larabell, Lynn Melnick, Todd Shalom, and Matvei Yankelevich.

Thank you to Ryan Murphy and everyone at Four Way Books, and, always and especially, to Darcie Dennigan and Kate Schapira, without whose brilliance, commiseration, and expert editing I'd be lost.

Many of these poems were written under the influence of John Berger's *And Our Faces, My Heart, Brief as Photos* and I will be forever sorry that I didn't get to talk to him about it and everything else that is or might be the case.

With all my love, this book is for Willie, Maggie, and Rusty.

Kate Colby is the author of seven books of poetry. *Fruitlands* (Litmus Press 2006) won the Norma Farber First Book Award from the Poetry Society of America in 2007. She has been awarded fellowships from Rhode Island State Council for the Arts and Harvard's Woodberry Poetry Room and was a founding board member of the Gloucester Writers Center in Massachusetts, where she hosts an occasional reading series. She lives with her family in Providence.

Publication of this book was made possible by grants and donations. We are also grateful to those individuals who participated in our 2017 Build a Book Program. They are:

Anonymous (6), Evan Archer, Sally Ball, Vincent Bell, Jan Bender-Zanoni, Zeke Berman, Kristina Bicher, Laurel Blossom, Carol Blum, Betsy Bonner, Mary Brancaccio, Lee Briccetti, Deirdre Brill, Anthony Cappo, Carla & Steven Carlson, Caroline Carlson, Stephanie Chang, Tina Chang, Liza Charlesworth, Paula Colangelo, Maxwell Dana, Machi Davis, Marjorie Deninger, Emily Flitter, Lukas Fauset, Monica Ferrell, Jennifer Franklin, Helen Fremont & Donna Thagard, Robert Fuentes & Martha Webster, Chuck Gillett, Dorothy Goldman, Dr. Lauri Grossman, Naomi Guttman & Jonathan Mead, Steven Haas, Mary & John Heilner, Hermann Hesse, Deming Holleran, Nathaniel Hutner, Janet Jackson, Christopher Kempf, David Lee, Jen Levitt, Howard Levy, Owen Lewis, Paul Lisicky, Sara London & Dean Albarelli, David Long, Katie Longofono, Cynthia Lowen, Ralph & Mary Ann Lowen, Donna Masini, Louise Mathias, Catherine McArthur, Nathan McClain, Victoria McCoy, Gregory McDonald, Britt Melewski, Kamilah Moon, Carolyn Murdoch, Rebecca & Daniel Okrent, Tracey Orick, Zachary Pace, Gregory Pardlo, Allyson Paty, Veronica Patterson, Marcia & Chris Pelletiere, Maya Pindyck, Taylor Pitts, Eileen Pollack, Barbara Preminger, Kevin Prufer, Vinode Ramgopal, Martha Rhodes, Peter & Jill Schireson, Roni & Richard Schotter, Andrew Seligsohn, Soraya Shalforoosh, Peggy Shinner, James Snyder & Krista Fragos, Alice St. Claire-Long, Megan Staffel, Robin Taylor, Marjorie & Lew Tesser, Boris Thomas, Judith Thurman, Susan Walton, Calvin Wei, Abby Wender, Bill Wenthe, Allison Benis White, Elizabeth Whittlesey, Hao Wu, Monica Youn, and Leah Zander.

31192021591373